Flavors of Lima: A Culinary Journey Through Peru

Clock Street Books

Published by Clock Street Books, 2023.

FLAVORS OF LIMA: A CULINARY JOURNEY THROUGH PERU

First edition. June 19, 2023.

ISBN: 979-8223668411

Written by Clock Street Books.

Table of Contents

Introduction

Welcome to *Flavors of Lima: A Culinary Journey Through Peru.* In this cookbook, we invite you to embark on a gastronomic adventure through the vibrant and diverse cuisine of Lima, the capital city of Peru. Lima's culinary scene is a true reflection of Peru's rich cultural heritage, blending traditional Peruvian flavors with influences from Spanish, African, Chinese, and Japanese cuisines. It is a melting pot of flavors and techniques that have been passed down through generations, resulting in a culinary tapestry that is both exciting and captivating.

Lima, often referred to as the "Gastronomic Capital of South America," boasts a unique culinary landscape that has gained international recognition and acclaim. The city's geographical location along the Pacific coast provides an abundance of fresh seafood, while its proximity to the Andes Mountains offers a diverse range of high-quality ingredients such as potatoes, corn, and quinoa. These elements, combined with the creativity and passion of Lima's talented chefs, have elevated the city's cuisine to new heights.

Peruvian cuisine as a whole is known for its harmonious blend of flavors, vibrant colors, and diverse ingredients. It draws inspiration from the country's indigenous roots, Spanish colonization, African influences brought by slaves, and the waves of immigrants from China and Japan. Lima, being the cultural and culinary hub of Peru, has become the epicenter where these culinary traditions intertwine and flourish.

In this cookbook, we aim to showcase the essence of Lima's culinary heritage by presenting a collection of recipes that represent the city's iconic dishes, as well as its unique fusion cuisine. Each recipe has been carefully selected to provide you with a comprehensive understanding of Lima's culinary landscape, allowing you to recreate these flavors in your own kitchen.

We invite you to embrace the richness and diversity of Lima's culinary heritage. Through these recipes, we hope to transport you to the streets of Lima, where the aromas, flavors, and vibrant culture intertwine to create an unforgettable culinary experience. So, fasten your apron, sharpen your knives, and join us on this mouthwatering journey as we discover the flavors that define Lima's extraordinary cuisine. Let's get cooking!

Chapter 1: Lima's Culinary Heritage

Lima, the capital city of Peru, is not only known for its rich history and breathtaking architecture but also for its vibrant and diverse culinary scene. The cuisine of Lima reflects the city's unique cultural heritage, shaped by centuries of influences from various civilizations and immigrant communities. In this chapter, we will delve into the fascinating culinary history of Lima and explore the cultural influences that have shaped its distinctive flavors.

Lima's culinary story begins with its indigenous roots. Long before the arrival of the Spanish conquistadors, the region was inhabited by indigenous civilizations such as the Incas, who had a deep understanding of the land and its resources. These early inhabitants cultivated crops like corn, potatoes, and quinoa, which formed the foundation of their diet. The techniques and ingredients they used laid the groundwork for what would eventually become the diverse and flavorful cuisine of Lima.

With the arrival of the Spanish in the 16th century, Peru witnessed a profound culinary transformation. The Spanish conquistadors brought with them European ingredients and cooking techniques, which merged with the indigenous culinary traditions to create a fusion of flavors. This fusion gave birth to traditional Peruvian dishes that are still celebrated today, such as Causa Limeña, a layered dish of seasoned mashed potatoes with various fillings, and Aji de Gallina, a creamy chicken stew flavored with aji amarillo peppers.

During the colonial period, Lima became a melting pot of cultures due to its role as the administrative and commercial center of the Spanish empire in South America. African slaves were brought to Peru to work on sugar plantations and mines, and they brought with them their culinary traditions and flavors. The African influence can be seen in dishes like Seco de Cordero, a lamb stew seasoned with a blend of aromatic spices, and Tacu Tacu, a dish of rice and beans that reflects the resourcefulness and creativity born out of necessity.

In the 19th century, Chinese and Japanese immigrants arrived in Peru, particularly in Lima, seeking new opportunities. They brought with them their culinary techniques and ingredients, which further enriched Lima's culinary landscape. The fusion of Peruvian and Asian flavors gave rise to Nikkei and Chifa cuisines. Nikkei cuisine combines Japanese techniques with Peruvian ingredients, resulting in dishes like Tiradito Nikkei, a delicate preparation of thinly sliced fish dressed in a citrus-based sauce with a touch of soy. Chifa cuisine, on the other hand, blends Chinese and Peruvian flavors, evident in dishes like Arroz Chaufa, a Peruvian-style fried rice.

Essential Ingredients and Cooking Techniques

To fully appreciate Lima's cuisine, it is essential to familiarize ourselves with the ingredients and cooking techniques that define its flavors. Lima's geographical location along the Pacific coast offers a bountiful supply of fresh seafood, which forms the backbone of many traditional dishes. From the prized sea bass used in Ceviche Limeño, a refreshing dish of fish marinated in tangy lime juice, to the succulent shrimp found in Arroz con Mariscos, a flavorful seafood rice dish, seafood plays a prominent role in Lima's culinary repertoire.

Potatoes, another staple ingredient, hold a special place in Peruvian cuisine, and Lima showcases the incredible diversity of potato varieties available in Peru. From the creamy yellow potatoes used in Papa a la Huancaina to the starchy potatoes used in Causa Limeña, each variety brings a unique texture and flavor to the dishes. Additionally, corn is another essential ingredient deeply intertwined with Peruvian cuisine. The large kernels of Peruvian corn are used in dishes like Anticuchos, grilled skewers of marinated beef heart, and Mazamorra Morada, a sweet and vibrant purple corn pudding.

Lima's cuisine is also characterized by its vibrant use of spices and peppers. Aji amarillo, a bright yellow chili pepper, is one of the most important ingredients in Peruvian cooking. It adds a distinct fruity heat to dishes and is featured prominently in dishes like Aji de Gallina. Other peppers like rocoto and aji panca are also commonly used, each contributing its unique flavor and spice level.

In terms of cooking techniques, one cannot overlook the significance of ceviche in Lima's culinary heritage. Ceviche is a beloved dish of fresh raw fish marinated in citrus juices, typically lime, which "cooks" the fish through a process called denaturation. The result is a refreshing and tangy dish that showcases the freshness of the seafood and the skill of the chef.

Another iconic cooking technique in Lima is the stir-fry method known as "saltado." Lomo Saltado, a classic dish, exemplifies this technique. It involves quickly stir-frying beef, onions, tomatoes, and soy sauce in a hot skillet, creating a flavorful and aromatic combination. This technique, influenced by Chinese culinary traditions, reflects the fusion of cultures that is prevalent in Lima's cuisine.

Traditional Peruvian Ingredients and Pantry Staples

To explore Lima's culinary heritage, it is important to have an understanding of traditional Peruvian ingredients and pantry staples. Here are some key ingredients you will encounter throughout this cookbook:

1. Aji Amarillo: A bright yellow chili pepper with fruity flavors and moderate heat. It is the backbone of many Peruvian dishes and adds a distinctive flavor.

2. Rocoto: A fiery red chili pepper with a floral and spicy flavor. It is often used in spicy sauces and stews.

3. Aji Panca: A dark red chili pepper with a smoky and fruity flavor. It is commonly used in marinades and sauces.

4. Huacatay: Also known as Peruvian black mint, huacatay leaves have a unique flavor reminiscent of mint and basil. They are used in marinades, sauces, and stews.

5. Choclo: Large-kernel Peruvian corn that is used in various dishes, both as a whole corn and as ground cornmeal.

6. Quinoa: A nutritious grain-like crop native to the Andean region. It is commonly used in salads, soups, and side dishes.

7. Huacatay: Also known as Peruvian black mint, huacatay leaves have a unique flavor reminiscent of mint and basil. They are used in marinades, sauces, and stews.

8. Huacatay: Also known as Peruvian black mint, huacatay leaves have a unique flavor reminiscent of mint and basil. They are used in marinades, sauces, and stews.

These ingredients, along with others like purple potatoes, lucuma fruit, and Peruvian corn beer (chicha), contribute to the vibrant and diverse flavors that define Lima's culinary heritage.

As we continue our culinary journey through Lima, we will explore these ingredients in detail and discover how they come together to create the iconic dishes that have captivated food lovers around the world.

In the next chapters, we will dive into the classic Lima dishes, fusion cuisine, street food delights, sweets and desserts, and signature Lima drinks. By the end of this cookbook, you will have a comprehensive understanding of Lima's gastronomy and be ready to embark on your own culinary adventures in your kitchen. So, prepare your taste buds and get ready to savor the incredible flavors of Lima's cuisine!

Chapter 2: Classic Lima Dishes

In this chapter, we will explore the classic dishes that have come to define Lima's culinary heritage. These iconic recipes capture the essence of Lima's gastronomy and are beloved by both locals and visitors alike. From the refreshing and tangy Ceviche Limeño to the flavorful and aromatic Lomo Saltado, each dish tells a story of Lima's cultural influences and culinary prowess. Join us as we embark on a culinary journey through the heart of Lima's classic cuisine. All recipes serve four people.

Ceviche Limeño

Ingredients:

- 1 pound fresh white fish fillets (such as sea bass or flounder), cut into bite-sized pieces

- 1 cup fresh lime juice

- 1 red onion, thinly sliced

- 1-2 aji amarillo peppers, seeded and finely chopped

- 1 garlic clove, minced

- 1 teaspoon salt

- 1 teaspoon freshly ground black pepper

- 1 tablespoon chopped fresh cilantro leaves

- 1 sweet potato, boiled and sliced

- 1 ear of corn, boiled and sliced

- Lettuce leaves, for serving

Instructions:

1. In a non-reactive bowl, combine the fish, lime juice, red onion, aji amarillo peppers, garlic, salt, and black pepper. Make sure the fish is fully immersed in the lime juice. Cover and refrigerate for about 20-30 minutes, or until the fish turns opaque and "cooks" in the lime juice.

2. Once the fish is ready, drain the excess lime juice. Add the chopped cilantro and toss gently to combine.

3. To serve, arrange lettuce leaves on a platter. Place the ceviche mixture on top of the lettuce leaves. Garnish with boiled sweet potato slices and boiled corn slices. Serve immediately and enjoy the refreshing flavors of Ceviche Limeño.

Lomo Saltado

Ingredients:

- 1 pound beef sirloin, cut into thin strips

- 1 red onion, cut into thick slices

- 2 tomatoes, cut into thick slices

- 1-2 aji amarillo peppers, seeded and cut into thin strips

- 3 tablespoons soy sauce

- 2 tablespoons red wine vinegar

- 2 garlic cloves, minced

- 1 teaspoon ground cumin

- 1 teaspoon paprika

- Salt and pepper, to taste

- 2 tablespoons vegetable oil

- 4 cups cooked rice

- French fries, for serving

Instructions:

1. In a bowl, combine the beef strips, soy sauce, red wine vinegar, garlic, cumin, paprika, salt, and pepper. Allow the beef to marinate for at least 15 minutes.

2. In a large skillet or wok, heat the vegetable oil over high heat. Add the marinated beef and stir-fry for 2-3 minutes, or until browned. Remove the beef from the skillet and set aside.

3. In the same skillet, add the onions, tomatoes, and aji amarillo peppers. Stir-fry for 2-3 minutes, or until the vegetables are slightly softened.

4. Return the beef to the skillet and stir-fry with the vegetables for an additional 1-2 minutes to combine the flavors.

5. Serve the Lomo Saltado over cooked rice and accompany it with crispy French fries. Enjoy this flavorful and satisfying dish that combines the best of Peruvian and Chinese influences.

Anticuchos

Ingredients:

- 1 pound beef heart, cut into bite-sized pieces
- 1/4 cup red wine vinegar
- 2 tablespoons soy sauce
- 2 tablespoons aji panca paste
- 2 garlic cloves, minced
- 1 teaspoon ground cumin
- 1 teaspoon dried oregano
- Salt and pepper, to taste
- Wooden skewers, soaked in water for 30 minutes

Instructions:

1. In a bowl, combine the red wine vinegar, soy sauce, aji panca paste, garlic, cumin, oregano, salt, and pepper. Mix well to create the marinade.

2. Add the beef heart pieces to the marinade, making sure each piece is well-coated. Cover and refrigerate for at least 1 hour, or preferably overnight to allow the flavors to meld.

3. Preheat a grill or grill pan to medium-high heat.

4. Thread the marinated beef heart pieces onto the soaked wooden skewers.

5. Grill the anticuchos for about 2-3 minutes per side, or until cooked to your desired level of doneness.

6. Serve the anticuchos hot as a delicious street food snack or as part of a main meal. They pair perfectly with aji sauce and a side of Peruvian potatoes.

Papa a la Huancaina

Ingredients:

- 4 large yellow potatoes, boiled and peeled

- 1 cup queso fresco (or feta cheese), crumbled

- 1/2 cup evaporated milk

- 3 tablespoons aji amarillo paste

- 2 tablespoons vegetable oil

- 4-6 saltine crackers

- Salt and pepper, to taste

- Lettuce leaves, for serving

- Black olives and hard-boiled eggs, sliced, for garnish

Instructions:

1. In a blender or food processor, combine the queso fresco, evaporated milk, aji amarillo paste, vegetable oil, salt, and pepper. Blend until smooth and creamy. If the sauce is too thick, add a splash of milk to thin it out.

2. Arrange the boiled potatoes on a bed of lettuce leaves on a serving platter.

3. Pour the huancaina sauce over the potatoes, ensuring that they are evenly coated.

4. Crush the saltine crackers into small crumbs and sprinkle them over the sauce.

5. Garnish with sliced black olives and hard-boiled egg slices.

6. Serve the Papa a la Huancaina as an appetizer or side dish, and savor the creamy and spicy flavors that make this dish a classic in Lima's culinary repertoire.

Tiradito

Ingredients:

- 1 pound fresh white fish fillets (such as flounder or sole), thinly sliced

- 1/4 cup freshly squeezed lime juice

- 2 tablespoons aji amarillo paste

- 1 tablespoon soy sauce

- 1 tablespoon olive oil

- 1 garlic clove, minced

- 1/2 teaspoon sugar

- Salt and pepper, to taste

- Fresh cilantro leaves, for garnish

- Thinly sliced red onion, for garnish

Instructions:

1. In a bowl, whisk together the lime juice, aji amarillo paste, soy sauce, olive oil, garlic, sugar, salt, and pepper to make the marinade.

2. Arrange the fish slices on a serving platter.

3. Pour the marinade over the fish, ensuring that each slice is coated. Let it marinate for 5-10 minutes to allow the flavors to meld.

4. Garnish with fresh cilantro leaves and thinly sliced red onion.

5. Serve the Tiradito chilled as a delicate and refreshing appetizer or light main course, and relish the delicate balance of flavors and textures.

Arroz con Mariscos

Ingredients:

- 2 cups long-grain white rice

- 1 pound mixed seafood (such as shrimp, mussels, squid, and fish fillets), cleaned and deveined

- 1 onion, finely chopped

- 2 garlic cloves, minced

- 1 red bell pepper, diced

- 1 cup frozen peas

- 1 tablespoon aji amarillo paste

- 1 teaspoon ground cumin

- 1 teaspoon paprika

- 2 cups seafood broth or fish stock

- 1/4 cup white wine (optional)

- 2 tablespoons vegetable oil

- Salt and pepper, to taste

- Fresh cilantro leaves, for garnish

- Lime wedges, for serving

Instructions:

1. Rinse the rice under cold water until the water runs clear. Drain well.

2. In a large pot or Dutch oven, heat the vegetable oil over medium heat. Add the chopped onion, minced garlic, and diced red bell pepper. Sauté until the vegetables are softened and aromatic.

3. Add the aji amarillo paste, ground cumin, and paprika. Stir well to coat the vegetables.

4. Add the rice to the pot and stir to combine with the vegetables and spices.

5. Pour in the seafood broth and white wine (if using). Season with salt and pepper to taste. Bring the mixture to a boil, then reduce the heat to low, cover, and simmer for 15-20 minutes, or until the rice is cooked and the liquid has been absorbed.

6. Meanwhile, in a separate skillet, heat a bit of oil over medium heat. Add the seafood and sauté until cooked through. Season with salt and pepper.

7. Once the rice is cooked, fluff it with a fork and gently fold in the cooked seafood and frozen peas.

8. Garnish with fresh cilantro leaves and serve the Arroz con Mariscos with lime wedges on the side. Enjoy the flavorsome and aromatic seafood rice dish that showcases the bountiful offerings of the sea.

Chapter 3: Fusion Cuisine

Lima's culinary landscape is a testament to the city's rich history of cultural influences and cross-cultural exchanges. In this chapter, we delve into the world of fusion cuisine, where traditional Peruvian flavors intertwine with culinary traditions from around the world. From the delicate artistry of Nikkei cuisine, blending Japanese and Peruvian flavors, to the bold flavors of Chifa cuisine, fusing Peruvian and Chinese culinary techniques, and the soulful creations of Afro-Peruvian cuisine, we explore the incredible fusion dishes that have become an integral part of Lima's gastronomy. Additionally, we will also discover vegetarian and vegan adaptations of traditional Peruvian dishes, ensuring that everyone can savor the diverse flavors of Lima's fusion cuisine. All recipes serve four people.

Tiradito Nikkei

Ingredients:

- 1 pound fresh white fish fillets (such as flounder or sole), thinly sliced

- 1/4 cup freshly squeezed lime juice

- 2 tablespoons soy sauce

- 1 tablespoon sesame oil

- 1 tablespoon aji amarillo paste

- 1 tablespoon honey
- 1 teaspoon grated ginger
- 1 garlic clove, minced
- Salt and pepper, to taste
- Fresh cilantro leaves, for garnish
- Thinly sliced green onions, for garnish
- Toasted sesame seeds, for garnish

Instructions:

1. In a bowl, whisk together the lime juice, soy sauce, sesame oil, aji amarillo paste, honey, grated ginger, minced garlic, salt, and pepper to make the marinade.

2. Arrange the fish slices on a serving platter.

3. Pour the marinade over the fish, ensuring that each slice is coated. Let it marinate for 5-10 minutes to allow the flavors to meld.

4. Garnish with fresh cilantro leaves, thinly sliced green onions, and toasted sesame seeds.

5. Serve the Tiradito Nikkei chilled as a stunning and flavorful appetizer or light main course, and appreciate the harmonious blend of Japanese and Peruvian influences.

Maki Acevichado

Ingredients:

- 2 cups sushi rice

- 4 nori seaweed sheets

- 1/2 pound fresh white fish fillets (such as flounder or sole), thinly sliced

- 1 avocado, sliced

- 1/4 cup aji amarillo mayo (mix aji amarillo paste with mayonnaise)

- 2 tablespoons toasted sesame seeds

- Soy sauce, for serving

- Pickled ginger, for serving

- Wasabi, for serving

Instructions:

1. Prepare the sushi rice according to package instructions and let it cool to room temperature.

2. Place a sheet of nori on a bamboo sushi mat or a clean kitchen towel.

3. Spread a thin layer of sushi rice evenly over the nori, leaving a small border along the edges.

4. Lay the sliced fish and avocado slices on top of the rice.

5. Drizzle the aji amarillo mayo over the fish and avocado.

6. Starting from one end, tightly roll the sushi using the bamboo mat or kitchen towel, applying gentle pressure to secure the filling.

7. Once rolled, sprinkle the toasted sesame seeds over the outside of the roll and press gently to adhere.

8. Repeat the process with the remaining ingredients.

9. Using a sharp knife, slice the sushi roll into bite-sized pieces.

10. Serve the Maki Acevichado with soy sauce, pickled ginger, and wasabi on the side. Enjoy this creative fusion of Peruvian and Japanese flavors in a delightful sushi roll.

Arroz Chaufa

Ingredients:

- 2 cups cooked white rice, chilled

- 1/2 pound boneless, skinless chicken breasts, cut into small pieces

- 1/2 cup cooked shrimp, peeled and deveined

- 1/2 cup diced ham

- 1/2 cup frozen peas

- 1/2 cup diced carrots

- 1/2 cup diced red bell pepper

- 3 tablespoons soy sauce

- 2 tablespoons vegetable oil

- 2 cloves garlic, minced

- 2 eggs, beaten

- Salt and pepper, to taste

- Green onions, sliced, for garnish

Instructions:

1. Heat the vegetable oil in a large skillet or wok over medium-high heat.

2. Add the minced garlic and sauté for about 30 seconds, until fragrant.

3. Add the chicken pieces and cook until they are no longer pink.

4. Push the cooked chicken to one side of the pan and add the beaten eggs to the other side. Scramble the eggs until fully cooked.

5. Add the cooked shrimp, diced ham, frozen peas, diced carrots, and diced red bell pepper to the pan. Stir-fry for a few minutes until the vegetables are tender-crisp.

6. Add the chilled rice to the pan and break up any clumps with a spatula.

7. Pour the soy sauce over the rice and stir-fry for another few minutes until the rice is heated through and well-coated in the soy sauce.

8. Season with salt and pepper to taste.

9. Garnish with sliced green onions and serve the Arroz Chaufa hot as a satisfying and flavorful fusion dish that combines the best of Peruvian and Chinese culinary traditions.

Seco de Cordero

Ingredients:

- 2 pounds lamb shoulder, cut into chunks

- 1 cup beer (such as lager or pilsner)

- 1 cup beef broth

- 1/2 cup chopped red onion

- 1/4 cup chopped cilantro

- 2 garlic cloves, minced

- 2 tablespoons vegetable oil

- 2 tablespoons aji panca paste

- 1 tablespoon ground cumin

- 1 tablespoon dried oregano

- 2 cups frozen green peas

- Salt and pepper, to taste

- Cooked white rice, for serving

Instructions:

1. In a large bowl, combine the lamb shoulder chunks, beer, beef broth, chopped red onion, chopped cilantro, minced garlic, aji panca paste, ground cumin, dried oregano, salt, and pepper. Mix

well to ensure the meat is coated in the marinade. Cover and refrigerate for at least 2 hours, or preferably overnight.

2. Heat the vegetable oil in a large pot or Dutch oven over medium-high heat.

3. Remove the marinated lamb from the bowl, reserving the marinade, and add it to the hot pot. Brown the lamb on all sides until it develops a rich caramelized crust.

4. Pour the reserved marinade into the pot, along with any remaining marinade ingredients.

5. Bring the mixture to a boil, then reduce the heat to low, cover, and simmer for 1 1/2 to 2 hours, or until the lamb is tender and the flavors have melded together.

6. Stir in the frozen green peas and simmer for an additional 5-10 minutes, until they are heated through.

7. Adjust the seasoning with salt and pepper to taste.

8. Serve the Seco de Cordero hot over cooked white rice, and savor the succulent and aromatic flavors of this Afro-Peruvian fusion dish.

Tacu Tacu

Ingredients:

- 2 cups cooked white rice, chilled

- 1 cup cooked canary beans or black beans

- 1/2 cup diced cooked ham

- 1/2 cup diced red onion

- 2 garlic cloves, minced

- 2 tablespoons vegetable oil

- 1 tablespoon aji amarillo paste

- 1 teaspoon ground cumin

- 1/2 teaspoon smoked paprika

- Salt and pepper, to taste

- Fried eggs, for serving

- Sliced avocado, for serving

Instructions:

1. In a large bowl, combine the cooked white rice, cooked canary beans or black beans, diced ham, diced red onion, minced garlic, aji amarillo paste, ground cumin, smoked paprika, salt, and pepper. Mix well to combine all the ingredients.

2. Heat the vegetable oil in a large skillet over medium-high heat.

3. Add the rice and bean mixture to the hot skillet, pressing it down with a spatula to form a compact layer.

4. Cook for 5-7 minutes, or until the bottom is golden brown and crisp.

5. Carefully flip the Tacu Tacu using a large plate or lid to assist you, and cook for an additional 5-7 minutes on the other side until golden brown and crisp.

6. Serve the Tacu Tacu hot, topped with a fried egg and sliced avocado. Enjoy this comforting and flavorsome Afro-Peruvian dish with its delightful fusion of textures and flavors.

Vegetarian Lomo Saltado

Ingredients:

- 2 cups seitan or firm tofu, cut into strips

- 1 red onion, thinly sliced

- 1 tomato, cut into wedges

- 1 bell pepper, cut into strips

- 2 cloves garlic, minced

- 2 tablespoons soy sauce

- 2 tablespoons vinegar (such as apple cider or red wine vinegar)

- 1 tablespoon aji amarillo paste

- 1 tablespoon vegetable oil

- 1/2 teaspoon ground cumin

- Salt and pepper, to taste

- Fresh cilantro leaves, for garnish

- Cooked white rice, for serving

- French fries, for serving

Instructions:

1. In a small bowl, whisk together the soy sauce, vinegar, aji amarillo paste, ground cumin, salt, and pepper to make the marinade.

2. Place the seitan or tofu strips in a shallow dish and pour the marinade over them. Let them marinate for at least 15 minutes.

3. Heat the vegetable oil in a large skillet or wok over medium-high heat.

4. Add the minced garlic and sliced red onion to the hot skillet and sauté until the onion becomes translucent and fragrant.

5. Add the marinated seitan or tofu, along with the tomato wedges and bell pepper strips, to the skillet. Stir-fry for a few minutes until the ingredients are heated through and well-coated in the marinade.

6. Adjust the seasoning with salt and pepper to taste.

7. Garnish with fresh cilantro leaves.

8. Serve the Vegetarian Lomo Saltado hot over cooked white rice, accompanied by crispy French fries. Enjoy this plant-based adaptation of a beloved Lima classic that retains all the vibrant flavors and textures of the original dish.

Chapter 4: Street Food Delights

In the bustling streets of Lima, the aroma of sizzling meats and the enticing scent of freshly cooked dough fill the air. Street food in Lima is a vibrant tapestry of flavors, offering a delightful glimpse into the city's culinary culture. From mouthwatering sandwiches to savory skewers and sweet treats, Lima's street food scene is a treasure trove of culinary delights. In this chapter, we'll explore some of the most beloved street food dishes that have captured the hearts and palates of locals and visitors alike. Get ready to indulge in the irresistible flavors of Pan con Chicharrón, Butifarra, Anticuchos de Pollo, Picarones, and Tamales as we delve into the world of Lima's street food scene. All recipes serve four people.

Pan con Chicharrón

Ingredients:

- 4 soft bread rolls or ciabatta buns

- 1 pound pork shoulder, thinly sliced

- 1 sweet potato, boiled and sliced

- 1 red onion, thinly sliced

- 1 tomato, thinly sliced

- 1/4 cup chopped cilantro

- 2 tablespoons lime juice

- 2 tablespoons mayonnaise

- 1 tablespoon aji amarillo paste

- Salt and pepper, to taste

Instructions:

1. Preheat the oven to 375°F (190°C).

2. Season the pork slices with salt and pepper.

3. Heat a skillet over medium-high heat and cook the pork slices until crispy and cooked through.

4. In a small bowl, combine the lime juice, mayonnaise, aji amarillo paste, salt, and pepper to make the sauce.

5. Slice the bread rolls or ciabatta buns in half and spread the sauce on both sides.

6. Layer the cooked pork slices, sweet potato slices, red onion, tomato, and chopped cilantro on the bottom half of the bread.

7. Place the sandwiches on a baking sheet and bake in the preheated oven for 5-7 minutes until warmed through.

8. Remove from the oven and cover with the top half of the bread.

9. Serve the Pan con Chicharrón hot and enjoy the delightful combination of crispy pork, sweet potato, and vibrant salsa criolla.

Butifarra

Ingredients:

- 4 soft bread rolls or ciabatta buns

- 8 slices of cooked ham

- 8 slices of roasted pork or tenderloin

- 1 red onion, thinly sliced

- 1 tomato, thinly sliced

- 1/4 cup chopped cilantro

- 2 tablespoons lime juice

- 2 tablespoons mayonnaise

- Salt and pepper, to taste

Instructions:

1. Preheat the oven to 375°F (190°C).

2. Slice the bread rolls or ciabatta buns in half and place them on a baking sheet.

3. In a small bowl, combine the lime juice, mayonnaise, salt, and pepper to make the sauce.

4. Spread the sauce on both sides of the bread.

5. Layer the ham slices, roasted pork or tenderloin slices, red onion, tomato, and chopped cilantro on the bottom half of the bread.

6. Place the sandwiches in the preheated oven for 5-7 minutes until warmed through.

7. Remove from the oven and cover with the top half of the bread.

8. Serve the Butifarra hot, savoring the delicious combination of flavors from the roasted pork, ham, and tangy salsa criolla.

Anticuchos de Pollo

Ingredients:

- 1 pound boneless, skinless chicken breasts, cut into chunks

- 1/4 cup vinegar (such as apple cider or red wine vinegar)

- 2 tablespoons aji panca paste

- 2 tablespoons vegetable oil

- 2 cloves garlic, minced

- 1 teaspoon ground cumin

- 1 teaspoon dried oregano

- Salt and pepper, to taste

- Wooden skewers, soaked in water for 30 minutes

Instructions:

1. In a bowl, combine the vinegar, aji panca paste, vegetable oil, minced garlic, ground cumin, dried oregano, salt, and pepper to make the marinade.

2. Add the chicken chunks to the marinade and coat them well. Allow the chicken to marinate for at least 1 hour, or preferably overnight in the refrigerator.

3. Preheat a grill or grill pan over medium-high heat.

4. Thread the marinated chicken chunks onto the soaked wooden skewers.

5. Grill the skewers for 10-12 minutes, turning occasionally, until the chicken is cooked through and has a slight char on the outside.

6. Serve the Anticuchos de Pollo hot and savor the succulent and flavorful grilled chicken skewers that are a popular street food delicacy in Lima.

Picarones

Ingredients:

- 1 cup all-purpose flour
- 1 cup pumpkin puree
- 1 cup sweet potato puree
- 1 teaspoon active dry yeast
- 1/2 teaspoon ground cinnamon
- 1/4 teaspoon ground cloves
- 1/4 teaspoon ground nutmeg
- 1/4 teaspoon salt
- Vegetable oil, for frying
- Syrup (chancaca or molasses-based syrup), for drizzling

Instructions:

1. In a large bowl, combine the all-purpose flour, pumpkin puree, sweet potato puree, yeast, ground cinnamon, ground cloves, ground nutmeg, and salt. Mix until a smooth batter forms.

2. Cover the bowl with a clean kitchen towel and let the batter rise in a warm place for about 1 hour, or until it has doubled in size.

3. In a deep skillet or pot, heat vegetable oil over medium heat to about 350°F (175°C).

4. Using a spoon or your hands, drop spoonfuls of the batter into the hot oil, forming small rings or doughnuts.

5. Fry the picarones until golden brown on both sides, turning them with a slotted spoon to ensure even cooking.

6. Remove the picarones from the oil and place them on a paper towel-lined plate to drain excess oil.

7. Drizzle the warm picarones with syrup (chancaca or molasses-based syrup) before serving.

8. Serve the Picarones as a delightful sweet street food treat, enjoying their crispy exterior and soft, flavorful interior.

Tamales

Ingredients:

- 2 cups masa harina (corn flour)

- 1 1/2 cups warm water or vegetable broth

- 1/2 cup vegetable shortening or lard

- 1 teaspoon baking powder

- 1/2 teaspoon salt

- Filling options: shredded chicken, pork, or beef; sautéed vegetables; or cheese

- Banana leaves or corn husks, soaked in warm water and cleaned

Instructions:

1. In a large mixing bowl, combine the masa harina, warm water or vegetable broth, vegetable shortening or lard, baking powder, and salt. Mix until a soft dough forms.

2. Take a soaked banana leaf or corn husk and spread a thin layer of the dough onto the leaf or husk.

3. Place a spoonful of your desired filling in the center of the dough.

4. Fold the sides of the leaf or husk over the filling to enclose it, forming a rectangular or square package.

5. Repeat the process with the remaining dough and filling.

6. Steam the tamales in a steamer basket or pot for about 45-60 minutes, or until the dough is firm and cooked through.

7. Remove the tamales from the steamer and let them cool slightly before unwrapping.

8. Serve the Tamales warm, unwrapped from the banana leaves or corn husks, and enjoy the traditional Peruvian corn-based dumplings filled with your favorite ingredients.

Chapter 5: Sweets and Desserts

No culinary journey through Lima is complete without indulging in the city's delectable array of sweets and desserts. Lima's desserts are a delightful blend of traditional flavors and creative twists, showcasing the richness of Peruvian ingredients and culinary traditions. From velvety and decadent creations to delicate treats bursting with flavor, Lima's dessert offerings are sure to satisfy any sweet tooth. In this chapter, we will explore some of the most beloved sweet treats of Lima, including Suspiro Limeño, Alfajores, Mazamorra Morada, Picarones con Miel, and Lucuma Ice Cream. Prepare to tantalize your taste buds and embark on a journey of sweet indulgence. All recipes serve four people.

Suspiro Limeño

Ingredients:

- 1 can (14 oz) condensed milk

- 1 can (14 oz) evaporated milk

- 4 egg yolks

- 1/2 cup granulated sugar

- 1 teaspoon vanilla extract

- 4 egg whites

- Ground cinnamon, for garnish

Instructions:

1. In a medium saucepan, combine the condensed milk, evaporated milk, egg yolks, and sugar. Whisk until well combined.

2. Place the saucepan over medium heat and cook the mixture, stirring continuously, until it thickens and coats the back of a spoon. This may take about 15-20 minutes.

3. Remove the saucepan from the heat and stir in the vanilla extract.

4. In a separate bowl, beat the egg whites until stiff peaks form.

5. Gently fold the beaten egg whites into the thickened milk mixture.

6. Pour the mixture into individual serving dishes or one large dish.

7. Sprinkle ground cinnamon on top for garnish.

8. Refrigerate for at least 2 hours before serving.

9. Serve the Suspiro Limeño chilled and revel in its luscious combination of dulce de leche and meringue.

Alfajores

Ingredients:

- 1 1/2 cups all-purpose flour

- 1/2 cup cornstarch

- 1/4 teaspoon baking powder

- 1/2 cup unsalted butter, softened

- 1/4 cup powdered sugar

- 1 teaspoon vanilla extract

- Dulce de leche, for filling

- Powdered sugar, for dusting

Instructions:

1. Preheat the oven to 350°F (175°C).

2. In a bowl, whisk together the all-purpose flour, cornstarch, and baking powder.

3. In a separate bowl, cream together the softened butter, powdered sugar, and vanilla extract until light and fluffy.

4. Gradually add the flour mixture to the butter mixture, mixing until a soft dough forms.

5. Roll out the dough on a lightly floured surface to a thickness of about 1/4 inch.

6. Cut out small rounds using a cookie cutter and place them on a baking sheet lined with parchment paper.

7. Bake the cookies in the preheated oven for 10-12 minutes, or until the edges are lightly golden.

8. Remove the cookies from the oven and let them cool completely.

9. Spread a generous amount of dulce de leche on the bottom side of one cookie and sandwich it with another cookie.

10. Repeat the process with the remaining cookies.

11. Dust the Alfajores with powdered sugar before serving.

12. Enjoy these delicate shortbread cookies with their irresistibly sweet dulce de leche filling.

Mazamorra Morada

Ingredients:

- 2 cups purple corn flour

- 8 cups water

- 1 cinnamon stick

- 4 cloves

- 1 cup diced pineapple

- 1 cup diced dried fruits (such as apricots, prunes, or raisins)

- 1 cup diced sweet potato

- 1/2 cup sugar

- Juice of 2 limes

- Ground cinnamon, for garnish

Instructions:

1. In a large pot, combine the purple corn flour and water. Stir until well mixed.

2. Add the cinnamon stick and cloves to the pot.

3. Bring the mixture to a boil, then reduce the heat and simmer for 30 minutes, stirring occasionally.

4. Add the diced pineapple, dried fruits, sweet potato, and sugar to the pot.

5. Continue to simmer for another 30 minutes, or until the sweet potato is tender and the mixture has thickened.

6. Remove the pot from the heat and stir in the lime juice.

7. Allow the Mazamorra Morada to cool before refrigerating for at least 2 hours.

8. Serve the Mazamorra Morada chilled, garnished with ground cinnamon.

9. Enjoy the sweet and vibrant flavors of this traditional purple corn pudding.

Picarones con Miel

Ingredients:

- 2 cups all-purpose flour

- 1 cup sweet potato puree

- 1 cup pumpkin puree

- 1 teaspoon active dry yeast

- 1/2 teaspoon ground cinnamon

- 1/4 teaspoon ground cloves

- 1/4 teaspoon ground nutmeg

- Vegetable oil, for frying

- 1 cup chancaca syrup or molasses-based syrup

Instructions:

1. In a large bowl, combine the all-purpose flour, sweet potato puree, pumpkin puree, yeast, ground cinnamon, ground cloves, and ground nutmeg. Mix until a smooth batter forms.

2. Cover the bowl with a clean kitchen towel and let the batter rise in a warm place for about 1 hour, or until it has doubled in size.

3. In a deep skillet or pot, heat vegetable oil over medium heat to about 350°F (175°C).

4. Using a spoon or your hands, drop spoonfuls of the batter into the hot oil, forming small rings or doughnuts.

5. Fry the picarones until golden brown on both sides, turning them with a slotted spoon to ensure even cooking.

6. Remove the picarones from the oil and place them on a paper towel-lined plate to drain excess oil.

7. Serve the Picarones warm, drizzled with chancaca syrup or molasses-based syrup.

8. Enjoy these Peruvian-style fritters with their sweet and syrupy goodness.

Lucuma Ice Cream

Ingredients:

- 2 cups heavy cream

- 1 cup whole milk

- 3/4 cup granulated sugar

- 4 egg yolks

- 1 teaspoon vanilla extract

- 1 cup lucuma pulp (can be found in specialty Latin American markets or online)

Instructions:

1. In a saucepan, combine the heavy cream and whole milk. Heat over medium heat until it reaches a simmer. Remove from heat and set aside.

2. In a bowl, whisk together the granulated sugar and egg yolks until well combined and slightly thickened.

3. Slowly pour the hot cream mixture into the egg yolk mixture, whisking constantly.

4. Return the mixture to the saucepan and cook over low heat, stirring continuously, until the custard thickens and coats the back of a spoon. Do not let it boil.

5. Remove the saucepan from the heat and stir in the vanilla extract and lucuma pulp. Mix until well incorporated.

6. Allow the mixture to cool to room temperature, then cover and refrigerate for at least 4 hours or overnight.

7. Pour the chilled mixture into an ice cream maker and churn according to the manufacturer's instructions.

8. Once the ice cream reaches a soft-serve consistency, transfer it to a lidded container and freeze for an additional 2-3 hours, or until firm.

9. Serve the Lucuma Ice Cream in bowls or cones, savoring the creamy and delicious flavors of Peru's beloved lucuma fruit.

Chapter 6: Signature Lima Drinks

Lima offers a delightful array of beverages that reflect the city's cultural heritage, traditions, and unique flavors. From the iconic Pisco Sour to the refreshing Chicha Morada, the beloved Inca Kola, the popular Cusqueña Beer, and the healthful Emoliente, these signature drinks are an essential part of the Lima culinary experience. In this chapter, we will dive into the recipes and stories behind these quintessential Lima drinks. So, raise a glass and let's toast to the tantalizing flavors of Lima!

Pisco Sour

Ingredients:

- 2 ounces pisco

- 1 ounce freshly squeezed lime juice

- 1 ounce simple syrup

- 1 egg white

- Ice cubes

- Angostura bitters, for garnish

Instructions:

1. In a cocktail shaker, combine the pisco, lime juice, simple syrup, and egg white.

2. Add a handful of ice cubes to the shaker and shake vigorously for about 15-20 seconds to froth the egg white.

3. Strain the mixture into a chilled glass.

4. Garnish with a few dashes of Angostura bitters on top.

5. Serve the Pisco Sour immediately and enjoy this iconic Peruvian cocktail.

Chicha Morada

Ingredients:

- 6 cups water

- 2 cups purple corn kernels

- 1 cinnamon stick

- 3 cloves

- 1 pineapple, peeled and diced

- 1 apple, peeled and diced

- 1 orange, juiced

- 1/4 cup sugar (adjust to taste)

- Lime wedges, for garnish

Instructions:

1. In a large pot, combine the water, purple corn kernels, cinnamon stick, and cloves.

2. Bring the mixture to a boil, then reduce the heat to low and simmer for about 45 minutes to 1 hour, or until the corn kernels are tender and the water turns a deep purple color.

3. Remove the pot from the heat and strain the liquid into a separate container, discarding the corn kernels and spices.

4. Place the strained liquid back into the pot and add the diced pineapple, apple, orange juice, and sugar.

5. Stir well to combine, then return the pot to the heat and simmer for another 10-15 minutes, or until the fruits are tender and the flavors are well infused.

6. Remove from heat and let the Chicha Morada cool.

7. Refrigerate for at least 2 hours before serving.

8. Serve the Chicha Morada chilled, garnished with lime wedges.

9. Enjoy this refreshing and vibrant purple corn-based beverage.

Inca Kola

Ingredients:

- 2 cups water

- 1 cup sugar

- 2 teaspoons lemon zest

- 2 teaspoons orange zest

- 1 teaspoon lemon extract

- 1 teaspoon orange extract

- 1/2 teaspoon yellow food coloring (optional)

- 1/2 teaspoon lemon juice

- 1/2 teaspoon orange juice

- 1 teaspoon citric acid (optional)

- 1 teaspoon quinine powder (optional)

Instructions:

1. In a saucepan, combine the water, sugar, lemon zest, and orange zest.

2. Bring the mixture to a boil, stirring until the sugar is dissolved.

3. Remove the saucepan from the heat and let the mixture cool.

4. Once cooled, add the lemon extract, orange extract, yellow food coloring (if using), lemon juice, orange juice, citric acid (if using), and quinine powder (if using).

5. Stir well to combine and dissolve any additional ingredients.

6. Transfer the mixture to a bottle or jug and refrigerate for at least 1 hour.

7. Serve the Inca Kola chilled in tall glasses or over ice.

8. Enjoy the unique and fruity flavors of Peru's beloved golden-colored soda.

Cusqueña Beer

Ingredients:

- Cusqueña beer (or your preferred Peruvian beer brand)

- Lime wedges, for garnish (optional)

Instructions:

1. Chill the Cusqueña beer in the refrigerator for a few hours.

2. Once chilled, pour the beer into glasses or mugs.

3. Optionally, garnish with lime wedges.

4. Serve the Cusqueña Beer immediately and enjoy its crisp and refreshing taste.

Emoliente

Ingredients:

- 4 cups water

- 1/4 cup dried horsetail

- 1/4 cup dried boldo leaves

- 1/4 cup dried alfalfa leaves

- 1 tablespoon dried linseed

- 1 tablespoon dried barley

- 1 tablespoon honey (optional)

- Lime juice or lemon juice, to taste

Instructions:

1. In a large pot, bring the water to a boil.

2. Add the dried horsetail, boldo leaves, alfalfa leaves, linseed, and barley to the boiling water.

3. Reduce the heat to low and simmer for about 10-15 minutes.

4. Remove the pot from the heat and let the mixture steep for another 5 minutes.

5. Strain the liquid into cups or mugs.

6. Add honey (if desired) and lime juice or lemon juice to taste.

7. Stir well to combine.

8. Serve the Emoliente warm and savor its herbal and soothing flavors.

9. Enjoy this traditional Peruvian herbal infusion drink believed to have various health benefits.

Conclusion: A Culinary Voyage through the Flavors of Lima

As we reach the end of our culinary journey through the vibrant cuisine of Lima, we can't help but reflect on the rich tapestry of flavors, influences, and traditions that make Lima a true gastronomic paradise. From the traditional dishes that showcase the city's culinary heritage to the innovative fusion creations that push the boundaries of taste, Lima's cuisine is a true reflection of its diverse cultural history and the creativity of its people.

Throughout this book, we have explored the various chapters that highlight the essence of Lima's culinary scene. We began with an introduction to Lima's rich culinary heritage, discovering the cultural influences and essential ingredients that shape the city's gastronomy. We then delved into classic Lima dishes, savoring the tangy and fresh Ceviche Limeño, the flavorful Lomo Saltado, the succulent Anticuchos, the creamy Papa a la Huancaina, the delicate Tiradito, and the aromatic Arroz con Mariscos. These dishes capture the essence of Lima's traditional cuisine, bringing to life the vibrant flavors and textures that define the city's culinary identity.

We then embarked on a journey through the world of fusion cuisine, exploring the captivating blend of flavors that result from the integration of different culinary traditions. Nikkei Cuisine introduced us to the delightful fusion of Japanese and Peruvian influences, while Chifa Cuisine brought together the flavors of Peru and China. We also discovered the Afro-Peruvian influences in dishes like Seco de Cordero and Tacu Tacu, celebrating the cultural diversity that shapes Lima's culinary landscape. Additionally, we explored vegetarian and vegan adaptations of traditional dishes, highlighting the adaptability and inclusivity of Lima's cuisine.

In the chapter on street food delights, we experienced the bustling energy of Lima's street food scene. From the irresistible Pan con Chicharrón to the flavorful Butifarra, the mouthwatering Anticuchos de Pollo, the sweet and indulgent Picarones, and the comforting Tamales, these street food delicacies captivate the senses and provide a glimpse into the vibrant street culture of Lima.

The chapter on sweets and desserts unveiled a world of indulgence and sweetness. From the luscious Suspiro Limeño to the delicate Alfajores, the vibrant Mazamorra Morada, the crispy Picarones con Miel, and the creamy Lucuma Ice Cream, Lima's desserts are a true celebration of flavors and textures, offering a sweet ending to any meal.

We then ventured into the world of signature Lima drinks, where we raised our glasses to the iconic Pisco Sour, the refreshing Chicha Morada, the beloved Inca Kola, the popular Cusqueña Beer, and the healthful Emoliente. These signature beverages are more than just drinks; they embody the spirit of Lima and provide a refreshing respite from the vibrant culinary experiences.

As we conclude this culinary voyage through the flavors of Lima, we are left with a deep appreciation for the city's gastronomic heritage and the talented chefs, cooks, and artisans who have preserved and evolved its culinary traditions. Lima's cuisine is a testament to the rich history, cultural diversity, and culinary innovation that define the city.

We hope this cookbook has inspired you to embark on your own culinary adventures, whether recreating the traditional dishes of Lima, exploring fusion creations, savoring street food delights, indulging in sweet treats, or toasting with signature drinks. We encourage you to continue exploring the vast and diverse world of Peruvian cuisine beyond the borders of Lima, discovering the regional specialties and hidden culinary gems that await.

May this book serve as your guide to the remarkable flavors of Lima, inviting you to embrace the culinary treasures of Peru and immerse yourself in a world of taste, culture, and tradition. So, gather your ingredients, sharpen your knives, and let your taste buds embark on a never-ending exploration of the gastronomic wonders that await you in Lima, Peru's culinary capital.

¡Buen provecho!

9 798223 668411

Printed by Libri Plureos GmbH in Hamburg,
Germany